Study Guide for Reading the BIBLE

the Law vol. 1

Study Guide for Reading the BIBLE

the Law vol. 1

THOMAS STANLEY JR.

iUniverse, Inc.
Bloomington

Study Guide for Reading the Bible the Law vol. 1

iUniverse books may be ordered through booksellers or by contacting:

iUniverse
1663 Liberty Drive
Bloomington, IN 47403
www.iuniverse.com
1-800-Authors (1-800-288-4677)

ISBN: 978-1-4620-2684-5 (sc)
ISBN: 978-1-4620-2685-2 (ebk)

Printed in the United States of America

iUniverse rev. date: 08/20/2011

Contents

I am Thomas (Tommy) Stanley Jr. I lived in Alabama for almost thirty-eight and half years. I have never been married, but I lived with my parents most of my life. I grew up in a Christian environment where I was raised up in a Christian family. I was called to preach the gospel when I was fifteen years old. Seven years ago I taught a Bible study class in the church that I attended (Mobile Revival Center Church). I used this information to teach the class.

In the future I want to be able to open up a church where I can preach the truth of the Word (which is the Message of the Cross) to a lost and dying world that needs Jesus. I have been to a church where the truth was preached in Baton Rouge, Louisiana.

I am currently working at Walmart in Semmes, Alabama as an overnight Dairy and Frozen Food stocking shelves. I have been there for seven years and enjoy working with the people I work with. I have worked in retail for nineteen years in stores like Delchamps Grocery and Food World. I just started writing this book when I was out of work for two years. I thought that the information I had gleaned many people might want to use because the students in my class still talk about how much they learned with this study.

Preface

Are you one of those people who have a problem reading the Word of God?· Then in this study you find it easy to read the Word. It is important if you are a new convert or a youth member that you read the Word of God. Many people will tell you read the gospel of John. I believe that is good when you first get saved. Later on you need to read the bible through from Genesis to Revelation that is when you can use this study to help you.

We have problems sometimes understanding the Word of God: or, We start reading the Word of God for a little time then we quit reading it because the bible gets boring or there is other things that we have to do right away. This study will help you to understand the Word of God and desire to read more then ever before.

I was teaching a class in our church this same study and each class member enjoyed it and could not wait for next week to continue with the study. Youth pastors and teachers should get one of these copies to r their class. When you do you will find that everyone in your class will enjoy the study the same way that my class enjoyed it. Thank you for taking time to check out this study: also, there will be more studies like this that I am publishing so you can continue teaching or doing this by yourself

Bible Study Questions in Genesis

Chapter 1

1) What is firmament in Genesis 1:6?

2) In verse 26 who does it talk about when it says "Let **us** make man in **our** image."?

3) What did God create in the six days he created?

Chapter 2

la) What is the name of the four rivers that border the Garden of Eden (where God placed man at)?

b) True or False. Was it one river that split into four heads.

2) What was the name of the tree that God forbid Adam to eat?

3) What did Adam say after God took a rib out of his body?

Chapter 3

1) True or False. Eve told the serpent that God said **we cannot even touch it lest ye die?**

2a) What was Eve's punishment that God gave her?

b) What was Adam's punishment?

3) What kind of angels did God place to guard the Garden of Eden (plus what else did they guard)?

Chapter 4

1) True or False. God brought the first fruits of his crop to offer unto God

2) Why did Cain say "Am I my brother's keeper" to God?

3) What did the Lord tell Cain after he made a statement in 4:14?

4) What was the occupation of Tubal-Cain?

5) Why did Lamech said if Cain would be avenged for his sevenfold then Lamech for seventy and sevenfold?

Chapter 5

I) Who was it that walked with God and was not?

2)Name the oldest man in the Bible and how old was he?

Chapter 6

1)Who are the sons of God in verse 2 and who are the daughters of men?

2)What did God create a flood on the earth?

3a)What kind of wood did Noah make the ark with?

b)What was the measurements of it?

c)True or False. There was only one story of the ark.

Chapter7

1)How many clean animals could Noah bring on the ark and How many unclean?

2)What was every substance that God destroyed?

3)How many days did the water prevail on earth?

Chapter 8

1) True or False The raven came back to the ark after Noah sent it out.

2) What did God say after he smelled a sweet savor?

Chapter 9

1)What did the Lord mean in verse 5?

2)What was the covenant God made in verse 11?

3)What did Noah 's two sons do with a garment?

4)What was the curse of Ham?

Chapter 10
l)What countries does Gomer and Magog represent?(who was the father of these two men?)

2)a What was the four cities Nimrod was ruler over?

b. True or False Ninevah was ruled by Nimrod.

3)True or False Sodom and Gomorrah were apart of Canaan.

Chapter 11
l)Was the earth with one language and one speech?

2)Who changed the speech of every person?

3)a True or False Haran died shortly after his father Terah.

b. Where was Terah when he died?

Chapter 12
I)Did God tell Abram to take Lot with him?

2)What did God say to Abram in verse 3?

3)Why did God plagued pharaoh and his house?

Chapter 13

1)What caused Lot to separate from Abram?(2reasons)

2)What did verse 13 talk about Sodom?

3)What did God say to Abram in verse 16?

Chapter 14

1)What was the name of the king that made war with Sodom and Gomorrah?

2)Who took Lot captive?

3)Abram sent who to take Lot back?

b. How many were there?

4)a Who gave the first tithes?

b. Who was it to?

Chapter 15
1)What did God say to Abram in verse I?

2)What happened to Abram when he slept?

3)What did God say to Abram in verse 13?(3things)

Chapter 16
1) What did Abram tell Sarai about her maid?

2) What two things was Hagar's son going to be?

3) What did Hagar call the Lord in verse 13?

Chapter 17

1) What did God tell Abram in verse 6? (2things)

2) What was the covenant in verse 1O? (describe it)

3) In verse 14, what will happen if they brake this covenant?

Chapter 18

1) What two comments did the Lord because of Sarah's laugh?

2) What will Abraham command his children and household to do? (2things)

3) What two questions did Abraham tell the Lord about Sodom and Gomorrah?

Chapter 19
l) What did the men do unto the men outside the door?

2) a. Wher did Lot want to go instead of the mountains?

b. Did the Lord agree to that what Lot said?

3) Did Lot go to Zoar or to a cave in the mountain?

b. What happened because he made the wrong decision in verse 31?

4) What was the tribe of Ben-ammi?

Chapter 20
1) What did God tell Abimelech in a dream?

2) What two reasons did he give him in verse 7?

3) What did God do to the house of Abimelech before Abraham prayed for him?

Chapter 21
1) What did Hagar see when God opened her eyes?

2) What did Abimelech make Abraham swear to do?

3)What was the reason Abraham gave him seven ewe lambs ?

Chapter 22
1)What did Isaac tell his father in verse 7?

2)Where was it that God told Abraham to do this?

3)Who was Rebekah's father and grandfather?

Chapter 23
1)What did Abraham tell the sons of Heth?

2)What was the name of the cave in verse 9?

3)How much did he pay for that land?

Chapter 24

1)How many thing; did the Lord bless Abraham?

2)What did Abraham tell his servant not to do?

3)What did the servant ask the Lord in his prayer?(4things)

4) a. Who is Rebekah's father and grandfather?

b. How is Abraham related to her grandfather?

c. What was the name of her brother?

5)What did he tell the servant ofAbraham?

6)What did Rebekah ' s family tell her?

Chapter 25
1)How much did Abraham give unto Isaac?

2)Did God bless Isaac before Abraham died?

3)What did the Lord tell Rebekah when she prayed to him?

4)Describe how the first child came out.

5)Why was Esau name called Edom?

Chapter 26

1) Where did the Lord tell Isaac not to go?

2) What did Abimelech tell his people?

3) Why did Isaac call the name of the well Rehoboth?

4) What was the covenant that Abimelech and Isaac made?

Chapter 27

1) How many goats did Rebekah tell Jacob to get?

2) What lie did Jacob tell his father about the venison?

3) What was Isaac blessing to Jacob?

4)What was Isaac blessing to Esau?

Chapter 28
1)When Esau seen Isaac didn't like his first wife what did he do?

2)What did Jacob dream?

3)What did the Lord tell him in verse IS?

4)What was the name of the city before it was called Bethel?

Chapter 29
1)What did Jacob do when he seen Rachel?(5things)

2) What ways did Jacob agree to work for Laban?

3) Why did Laban give Jacob his daughter Leah instead of Rachel?

4) a. What is the name of Leah's four sons?

b. What does each name represent? (research)

Chapter 30

1) What was Bilhah's two sons named?

b. What does each name represent?(research)

2) What was Zilpah's two sons named?

b. What does each name represent? (research)

3) What was Leah's other two sons and daugther called?

b. What does each name represent? (research)

4) What was the name Rachel's son?

b. What does his name represent?(research)

5) What did Jacob tell Laban what he wanted for his wages?

Chapter 31
1) What kind of dream did Jacob have?

2)What did Rachel steal?

3)What did God tell Laban in a dream ?

4)Did Jacob know what Rachel stole ?

5)What was the covenant Jacob and Laban made?

Chapter 32
1)Why did Jacob split his company into two groups?

2)What was the gift he was going to give his brother?

3)What did the angel wresting with Jacob do unto him?

4)What was Jacob's name changed to ?

5)What did the children of Israel not do in verse 32?

Chapter 33
1)How many times did he bow until he came near unto Esau?

2)What did Jacob tell Esau in verse 14?

3)Did he go with Esau to Seir?

Chapter 34
1)What did Shechem do unto Dinah?

2) Why were the sons of Jacob wroth?

3) What did they want Hamor, Shechem, and the other men in their city to do?

4) What Simeon and Levi do unto the men?

5) What did Jacob tell Simeon and Levi?

Chapter 35

1) Did Jacob's household get rid of their idols?

2) a. What was Rachel's other son called?

b. What does his name represent? (research)

3)Where was Rachel buried?

4)How old was Isaac when he died?

Chapter 36

l)a What was the name of Eliphaz's son?

b. Was this the tribe with the giants? (research)

2)a Were there kings in Edom before Israel?

b. What was the name of the eight kings?

Chapter 38
1)What did Shechem do unto Dinah?

2)Why were the sons of Jacob wroth?

3)What did they want Hamor, Shechem, and the other men in their city to do?

4)What Simeon and Levi do unto the men?

5)What did Jacob tell Simeon and Levi?

Chapter 39
1)Did Jacob's household get rid of their idols?

2)a What was Rachel's other son called?

b. What does his name represent?(research)

3)Where was Rachel buried?

4)How old was Isaac when he died?

Chapter 40
1)a What was the name of Eliphaz' s son ?

b. Was this the tribe with the giants? (research)

2)a Were there kings in Edom before Israe l?

b. What was the name of the eight kings?

b. The interpretation of it.

3)a. What was the dream the baker dreamed?

b. The interpretation of it.

4)a. Did the interpretations come to pass?

b. Did anyone of them remember Joseph?

Chapter 41
1)a. What was the first dream Pharoah dreamed?

b. The second dream.

2)Did the magicians and wisemen interpret the dreams?

3)a Did the two dreams have the same meaning?

b. What is the interpretation?

4)a Who did Pharoah put in charge of this?

b. What was the title he gave him?

c. How was he when he took over this title?

5)a What was the name of Joseph's first son?

b. What does his name represent? (research)

6)a What was the name of his second son?

b. What does his name represent? (research)

Chapter 42
l)Why did Jacob not send Benjamin with them?

2)What did he tell them in verse 19?

3)What did each of them find in their sacks?

Chapter 43

1) What did Judah tell his father in verse 9?

2) What did Joseph tell the ruler of his house?

3) How many times was Benjamin's food then the others?.

Chapter 44

1) Who's sack did Joseph tell his ruler to put his cup in?

2) What was going to happen to the one who had the cup?

3) What did Judah tell Joseph he would do?

Chapter 45

1)Was there someone around when he told his brothers who he was?

2)What reason did he tell them about them selling him?

3)How many years of famine was it in verse 6?

4)Where did he tell them that they would live?

5)What did Pharaoh tell Joseph about his family?

Chapter 46

1)What was the name of Levi's sons ?

2)How many of Jacob's family came to Egypt?

3)What did Joseph ask them to tell about their occupation?

Chapter 47
1)How old is Jacob?

2)What did Joseph tell the people they would have to give Pharaoh to get bread?

3)What did they give him the next year?(2things)

4)What was the law that was made by Joseph?

Chapter 48
1)What did Joseph do when Jacob was blessing Ephraim first ?

2) What comment did he give Joseph of this reason

3) What did he tell him in the last verse?

Chapter 49
1) What did Jacob tell Reuben should befall him?

2) What did he tell Simeon and Levi?

3) What did he tell Judah?(3things)

4) What did he tell Zebulun?

5) What did he tell Issachar?

6)What did he tell Dan?(2things)

7)What did he tell Gad?

8)What did he tell Asher?

9)What did he tell Naphtali?

10)What did he tell Joseph?(2things)

11)What did he tell Benjamin?

Chapter 50
1)Did Pharaoh let Joseph go but)' his father?

2)Did Joseph forgive his brethren for doing what they did to him?

3)What did Joseph tell his brethren?(2things)

Bible Study Questions in Exodus

Chapter 1
1. What does Exodus mean?

2. Did the new pharoah know Joseph?

3. What did Pharaoh say to his people about the Israelites?

4. What does rigor mean?

5. Did the two midwives do as pharoah commanded them?

6. What did pharoah tell his people in verse 22?

Chapter 2

1)Who was going to nurse the Hebrew baby for pharoah's daughter?

2)Why did Moses kill t he Egyptian?

3)What two questions did t he Hebrew men tell Moses?

4)Where did Moses flee to?

5)What was the name of Moses 's son?

Chapter 3

1)Was the bush that was on fire consumed?

2)Why did God tell Moses not to come near?

3)Name the six nations that live in the promise land.

4)What two questions did Moses tell God?

Chapter 4
l)a. What did the rod change into?

b.What happened when Moses told him to grab its tail?

2) a. What was the second thing God told him t o do?

b. What happened when he did this?

c .What happened when God told him to put his hand back?

3) Who was going to speak for Moses?

4) Why did God want to kill Moses?

Chapter 5
1) What did pharoah tell Moses and Aaron? (2things)

2) What did pharoah tell the tastmasters not to give t hem?

3) What two questions did Moses tell God?

Chapter 6
l) How old was Levi when he died?

2)a. What was the name of Moses and Aaron's father?

b. Name their grandfather.

3) What was the name o f Eleazar 's son?

Chapter 7
1) a. What was Aaron to Moses?

b. What does this mean?

2) What happened when the magicians of pharoah did the same thing?

b. Did Aaron's rod swallow thier rods?

3)What happened after the water was turned into blood? (3 things)

4)Did the magicians do the same thing?

5)What did the Egyptians do to find water?

Chapter 8

l)What was the second plague God judged Egypt with?

2)What are the places the frogs went in Egypt? (7 places)

3)Did the magicians do the same thing?

4)Did the Lord do as pharoah requested about getting rid of the frogs?

5) What happened to the land after they gathered up the frogs?

6) What was the third plague God judge d Egypt with?

7) Did the magicians do the same thing ?

8) What did t hey tell pharoah?

9) a. What was the fourth plague God judged Egypt with?

b. Did it have an affect on the Israelites?

Chapter 9
1) What was the fifth plague God judged Egypt with?

2) What does murrian mean?

3) Did any of the children of Israel's cattle die?

4)a. What was the sixth plague God judged Egypt with?

b. What cause d this plague?

5)What was the seventh plague God judged Egypt with?

6) Was there any hail like this ever in Egypt?

7) a. What did the hail destroy?(3things)

b. Did the Israelites have any hail?

Chapter 10

1) What was the eighth plague God judged Egypt with?

2) What places did they dwell in ? (3 places)

3) What caused the locusts to be in Egypt?

4) What two things did the locusts eat up?

5) a. What caused the locusts to leave Egypt?

b. Where did they go?

6) a. What was the ninth plague God judged Egypt with?

b. How many days did it last?

7) Did t he children of Israel have light?

Chapter 11
l) Was Moses great in the land of Egypt?

2) What was the tenth plague God judged Egypt with?

3) What shall the servants do unto Moses?

Chapter 12
l) a. What day and month was this done?

b. What shall they do?

2) What was proformed on the fourteenth day?

3) What is done with the remains of it?

4) Did God want them to keep this a memorial forever?

5) a. What does unleavened mean?

b. How many days should they keep this?

6) What will happen if they eat leaven in their bread?

7) Should they do this when they reach the promise land?

8) Why did pharaoh tell Moses and Aaron to take your people, flocks, herds, and go?

9) How many years were they in the l a n d of Egypt?

10) a. Was the stranger or hired servant able to protake of the pass **over?**

b. If so, what did they have to do?

11) What does the word passover mean?

Chapter 13
1) What shall they sanctify in verse 2?

2)What shall the fathers tell the sons?

3)Why didn't they go through the way of the philistines?

4)What did God led them with by day and night?

Chapter 14
1)What shall pharoah say of the children of Israel?

2) How many chariots pursued after them?

3) What two questions did they tell Moses?

4) Where did the pillar of cloud go?

5) What did God do to their chariots?

Chapter 15

l) What was the song Moses and the Israelites sung?

2) a. What did God do t o the Red sea in verse 8?

B. What does congealed mean?

3) What two questions did Moses say in verse 11?

4) What shall happen to Edom, Moab, Caanan? (5things)

5) Why couldn't they drink of the waters of Marah?

6) What caused them to be sweet?

7) What did Moses tell after this? (5reasons)

Chapter 16

1) Did the whole congregation murmur against them or just a few people?

2) a. What did God say unto Moses to prove unto them?

b. What shall they do on the sixth day?

3) When Aaron was speaking to the whole congregation what appeared in the wilderness?

4) What covered the camp at evening time?

5) a. What happened after t h e dew left in the morning?

b. What does manna mean?

6) What happened when they left it until the next morning?

7) Was there some people that gathered it on the third day?

8) Why did Aaron put a omer of manna in a pot?

Chapter 17

l) a. What two questions did Moses tell them?

b. What does chide mean?

2) What happened in Horeb?

3)What did Moses tell Joshua ? (2 things)

4)What happened in verse 11?

5)How did Aaron and Hur help Moses?.

Chapter 18
l) Who is Jethro to Moses?

2) What happened in the morning after he stayed the night with Jethro?

3) What did Jethro say unto Moses? (2 questions)

4) What did Moses tell him? (4 things)

5) What did Jethro say he should do? (4 things)

Chapter . 19

1)What month did they enter into the wilderness of Sinai?

2)Why did God tell Moses that He bore them on eagles's wings?

3) What does peculiar treasure mean?

4) a. What would happen to them if they went up to the mount or touched the border?

B. What was the punishment they would face?

Chapter 20

1) What does the word torah mean?

2) What was the first the commandment?

3)a. Name the second commandment.

b. What three places could they not make a graven image?

4) What does the word vain mean?

5) Who shouldn't work on the sabbath? (7 things)

6) What two things was God going to prove them with?

Chapter 21

1) On the seventh day what shall happen to the servant?

2) a. If the master give him a wife does he keep her?

b. What if the servant wants to stay?

3) How can she go free? (3 reasons)

4) What does guile mean?

5) What should happen to the man that hurts a person but doesn't kill him?

6) What would happen if the y hurt a woman with child?

7) a. What would happen to an ox if it kills a man or a woman?

b. What if the owner sees it pushing before it kills them?

8) What will happen if a man digs a pit an an another person's ox dies?(2things)

Chapter 22

1) What shall happen if a man steals a sheep to kill or sell it?

2) What will happen if his beast eats in someone else field?

3) a. Who will pay when they go before the judges in verse 9?

b. What shall they pay?

4) What shall a man do if he entices a virgin but the father refuses t o give her t o him?

5) What will happen to someone that affics a widow?

6) What shall they do with the flesh that was torn by beasts?

Chapter 23

l)How should they do unto an enemy's o x that is gone astray?

2)What can't they oppress a stranger?

3)What does circumspect mean in verse 13?

4)a .What is the three feasts they shall do?

b.Describe each o f them.

5)a.Who is the Angel in verse 20?

b.What two things shall He do?

6)What would happen if they didn't obey his voice?

7)What shall they do and not do to the six tribes in the promise land?(5things)

8)How shall he drive out the tribes?

9)What is the other reason that they are forbidden to do?

Chapter 24

1)Who went to worship God afar off?(5people)

2)Could they get near unto the Lord?

3)What vision did they see of God?

4) If any man had any problems who shall they go to?

5)What did the glory of the Lord look like?

6) How many days and nights was Moses on the mount?

Chapter 25

1)What offering did they have to give Moses?(15things)

2)What does sanctuary mean in verse 8?

3)What does the word ark mean?

4)Why shall the staves be placed in the rings of the ark?

5)What is the testimony they shall put in the ark?

6)a.What does mercy seat mean?

b.Why was it used?

7)Where did Moses go to commune with God?

8)What are the vessels on the table? (4things)

9) What is the showbread?

1 O) a.How many branches are on the candlestick?

b .How many lamps?

Chapter 26
l)How many curtains shall they make?

2)How many loops will it take to hold two curtains together?

3) Where shall the half curtain that remainth go?

4)What does the word tenon mean?

5)What shall the veil divide?

Chapter 27

l)What are the things that they shall use for sacrifices that are made of brass? (5things)

2)a . How long is the north and south sides?

b.How long is the west and east sides?

3)How long is the gate of the court?

4)Why shall they bring pure olive oil beaten?

5) a .What does the word statue mean?

b .Shall they do this forever?

Chapter 28

l)Name Aaron's four sons.

2) a.Who are the wisehearted?

b .What shall they do?

3) Describe the garments they shall make. (6things)

4)What is the curious girdle?

5) What shall they do with the onyx stones?

6)a .What shall be on the first row of stones?

b .On the second row.

c .On the third row.

d .On the fourth row.

7)a .What shall be in the breastplate?

b .What does both of them mean?

8)Why shall he have the s tones on his breastplate?

9)Why should he have a golden bell around the hem of his robe?

10)What shall Moses do to Aaron and his sons before they can minister? (3things)

Chapter 29

1)What is the first thing they shall do to be consecrated?

2)What shall they do with the blood? (2things)

3)What shall they do with the flesh and skin?

4)What is the second thing they shall do to be consecrated?

5) What shall they do with the blood?

6) What shall they with the whole ram?

7) What is the third they shall do to be consecrated?

8) What shall they do with the blood? (5things)

9) What is the fourth thing they shall do to be consecrated?

10) How many days shall the son wear the holy garments?

11) What shall they do with the remains of it that wasn't eaten?

12)What times shall they offer the two lambs?

Chapter 30
1)Where shall they put the alter of incense?

2) When shall Aaron burn the sweet incense?(2times)

3)How many times shall Aaron do this for an atonement?

4)What shall they give unto the Lord when Moses numbers them?

5) a . What is the age when they shall give?

b . Shall the rich give more or the poor give less?

6)Why shall they build a lavar and foot?

7)What shall they do with the anointed oil?(8things)

8)What will happen if they make the same oil or put it on a stranger?

9)What shall they do with the perfume they will make?

1O) What would happen if they make the same to smell?

Chapter 31
1) a .Who is Bezaleel`s father?

b .Name his grandfather.

c . What tribe are they from?

2 }What four things of the Spirit of God that was in him?

3) a . Who was the other person that worked with him?

b.What tribe was he from?

4)What was the punishment if they work the sabbath?

Chapter 32

l) Why did the people want to Aaron?(2reasons)

2)What did the people say after he made the calf?

3)What did Moses tell unto God?(3things)

4)a .What did he remind God of ?

b.Did God repent of what He was going to do them?

5)What did Joshua tell Moses that they sounded like or not like?(3things)

6)What did Moses do unto them the grounded up calf?

7)a.Who came to Moses when he said, "Who is the on the Lord`s sied?"

b .What did he tell them to do unto the ones who were not?(3things)

8) What did the Lord tell Moses about being blotted out of His book?

9)What was the punishment the Lord gave unto them?

Chapter 33

I)What did the people do when they heard the Lord tell Moses in verse 3?

2)Where did the people go to seek God?

3)How did the people react when they seen the cloudy pillar?

4)Why did Moses tell the Lord if His presence didn`t go with them to keep them there?

5)a .Where did the Lord tell Moses to go t o see His glory?

b .What did the Lord God show Moses?

Chapter 34

1)Who couldn`t come up with Moses to the mount?(3people)

2)What did the Lord say when He passed by Moses?(8things)

3)What was the covenant God made with Moses? (4 things)

4)What shall they not do in verse 25?(2things)

5)What did they put on his face so they could speak to him?

Chapter 35 , ..
1)Shall they kindle on the sabbath day?

2)Who shall give an offering unto the Lord?

3) a. What did the people bring unto Moses?(8things)

b. Who gave silver, brass, and shittem wood?

4) What did the woman who were wisehearted do?(2things)

5)What did the rulers bring?(4things)

Chapter 36
l)What did they bring unto Moses every morning?

2) a .What did the workers tell Moses?

b .What did Moses tell the people?

Chapter 37
1)Why did they put the staves into the rings by the sides of the ark?

2)What was the length of the altar of incense?

Chapter . 38
1)What is a basin?

2) a .What did he make the lavar and foot with?

b . What does that word mean?

3)Who was this in service for?

4)a .How much was the gold they occupied for the work?

b . How much was the silver?

5)How many men from 20 and up gave a half a shekel?

6) How much was the brass they occupied for the work?

Chapter 39
1)How did they work the linen into the ephod?

2) Why did they make a band around the hole?

Chapter . 40

1)What shall Moses do on the first day of the first month?

2)What shall their anointing be?

3)Why couldn`t Moses enter unto the tent of the congregation?

4)What did they do when the clould appeared or was taken up?

Bible Study Questions in Leviticus

Chapter 1

1) Where did the Lord speak to Moses?

2) What should the Israelites bring to offer unto the Lord ?(2things)

3) Narne the first offering that is in the book of Leviticus .

4) A.Shall the sacrifice be without blemish?

b. What does the word blemish mean?

c.How shall they offer it?

5)What does flay in verse 6 mean?

6)What do they do with the inwards and legs?(2things)

7)Do they divide the turtledove in asunder?

Chapter 2

1)Name the second offering that they did offer unto the Lord.

2)What shall they do with it?

3)What is the meaning ofrernnant in verse 3?

4)a.What does oblation mean? .

b.If they bring the meat offering baked in an oven, what shall it be?(2things)

5)Shall the meat offering be made ofleaven?

6)1s there to be salt on the meat offerings or not? , \

7)1f they offer the firstfruits for a meat offering,what shall they offer?

Chapter 3

1)Name the third offering they offered unto the Lord.

2)Describe how they offered it unto the Lord .

3)What shall they do with the inwards?(2things)

4)What is the other two things that are used for this sacrifice?

5)What does perpetual statute mean?

b.What shall they not eat?(2things)

Chapter 4

1)Does the priest that was anointed do the same sin as the people?

2)Name the fourth offering they offered unto the Lord.

3)What shall the priest do with blood?(4things)

4)Where shall he take the bullock?

b.What shall be poured out?

5)Why should they whole congregation offer for a sin offering?(5things)

6)What shall a ruler bring if he has sinned?

7)What kind of lamb shall they bring to offer?

Chapter 5
l)aWhat is the meaning of swearing?

b.How shall he bear someone else's iniquity?(2reasons)

2)Name the three unclean things that they couldn't touch.

b. What if someone else hides that person's sin?

3) What is an oath mean in verse 4?

b. What will happen if they swear with their lips and hide it from that person?

4) What shall they bring if they don't have an animal to bring to the sacrifice?

5) How much shall the priest burn on the altar?

6) What shall they bring if they commit a trespass? (2things)

7) How will his trespass be forgiven? (3reasons)

Chapter 6

I)What is the reasons for trespassing to their neighbor?(7reasons)

2)What shall he restore unto his neighbor?(5things)

3)How much else shall he give?

4)What is the law ofthe burnt offering?

5)Shall the fire upon the altar beput out?

6)What happens to the remainder of the meat offering?

7)Shall all the males ofthe children ofAaron eat it?

8)What is the offering they shall give when Aaron is anointed?

9)What if it is sodden in a brazen pot?(2things)

IO)What shall they do with the sin offering that was brought to the holy place for reconciliation?

Chapter 7
l)What is the law of the trespass offering?

2)What shall they offer if it is a thanksgiving?

3)What if it is a voluntary offering?

4)Shall they eat the flesh of the sacrifice on the third day?

b.What does imputed mean in verse 18?

c.What will happen if they eat on the third day?

5)What did the Lord tell them not to eat?(5things)

6)What did the Lord say about the wave breast&heave shoulder in verse 34?

Chapter 8
l)What did Moses tell the congregation in verse 5?

2)How many times did he sprink le the altar?

3)Why did Moses purify and sancify the altar?

A)What did Moses burn without the camp?(4things)

5)Why did Moses take them from their hands and burnt them?

6)What did Moses tell them in verse 33?

7)What shall they do in the seven days so they die not?

Chapter 9

I)What day did Moses call Aaron,his sons,and the elders?

2)What did Aaron tell them to bring?(4things)

3)What did the Lord command them to do so the glory can appear unto them?

4)What happened in verse 24?

Chapter 10
1)a.What didn't Nadab and Abihu take with them?(3things)

b.What kind of fire did they offer unto the Lord?

2)What caused them to die?

3)What did Moses tell Aaron that the Lord spoke ?

4)a.Who is Aaron's uncle?

b.What Moses tell the two men?

5)What did Moses tell Aaron and his sons they should do and not do?

6)What else did the Lord command Aaron and his sons not to do?

7)Why did he command them to do this?(3reasons)

8)What did Moses tell Eleazar and Ithamar in verse 17?

Chapter 11
1)What are the beasts that the children of Israel can eat?(2things)

2)What are the ones cannot eat and the reasons why they cannot eat them?(4things&4reasons)

3)What in the waters shall they eat?(2things)

4) What are the fowls that they shouldn't eat? (20 things)

5) What are the flying creeping thing they can eat? (4 things)

6) What will happen to the people that bear the carcasses?

7) What else shall be unclean of the creeping things to them? (8 things)

8) What did the Lord say in verse 44,45? (5 things)

9) Why did God make this a law?

Chapter 12
I) What will happen to a woman if she bears a son?

2)What will happen to her after the eighth day?

3)What if she bears a daughter?

Chapter 13

I)What if a man have leprosy in the skin of his flesh?(3places)

2)When shall the priest pronounce him unclean?

3)What the three steps to find that he is clean or unclean?

4)True or False If a man have raw flesh then he his clean.

5)What are the two steps to find out if the boil he has is clean or unclean?

6)What is it called if they have it in the beard or head?

7)What the three steps to determine if a person has leprosy in their beard?

8)What happens to the one with the bald head that has leprosy?(4things)

9)What if the garment has leprosy in it?(7things)

lO)If they find the plague what shall they do with it?

Chapter 14
I)What shall the priest command him to bring for cleansing?(4things)

2)What shall the priest do with the live bird ?(3things)

3)What shall he that is to be cleansed do?(5things)

4)\V.hat shall he do on the seventh day?(3things)

5)What shall the priest do with the remnant of oil left?

6)What will the owner of the house tell the priest?

7)Shall they empty their house before the priest goes into it?

8)What shall they do if there is a plague in their house?(5things)

9)What shall he do if the plague come back in the house?

1O)What does the word scruf mean?

Chapter 15
l)What is the uncleanness in his issue?(2things)

2)What are the things that are to be unclean?(2things)

3)What are the reasons that would make a person unclean?(6reasons)

b.What are the things they have to do to be cleansed?(3things)

4)What shall he do on the eighth day?

5)What does the word copulation mean?(research)

6)Shall every garment and skin be washed?

7)Why shall they separate from their uncleanness?

Chapter 16

l)What did the Lord tell Moses to speak unto Aaron after his two sons died?

2)What are the two lots that Aaron shall cast upon the goats?

3)What does scapegoat mean?(research)

4)What shall happen to the goat that fell to be the scapegoat?

5)Why shall Aaron put the incense upon before the Lord?

6)Who is it that the goat is offered for a sin offering?

7)What shall Aaron do unto the live goat?(4things)

8)Did it bear the inquities ofthe land not inhabited?

b.Who was it that beared the inquities ofthe land not inhabited?(how?)

9)What shall they do on the seventh month and tenth day ?(2things)

IO)What shall the priest that is anointed do?(7things)

Chapter 17
l)What will happen to the man that killeth animal and don' t bring it to be an offering?

2)What they no more offer their sacrifices unto?

3)What will happen if they eat any blood?

4)Why is this in verse II? . \

5)What shall they do who hunteth any beast that has been eaten?

6)What if he doesn't bathe his flesh?

Chapter 18
1)Shall they walk in their ordinances?

2)Recite verse 5 and what does this mean?(research)

3)How does this principle apply to us today?(research)

4)What does verse 6 mean?

5)Who is it that they can`t uncover their nakedness(18people)

6)What can't they do in verse 20?

7)What are the things they can't do in verse 21?(2things)

8)What does abomination mean?(research)

9)What is this called in verse 23?

b.What does the word confusion mean?

10)What did the Lord do to the nations before them?

11)How can we overcome these sins today?(research)

Chapter 19
1)What did the Lord tell them to do?(5things)

2)How should Christians reveal that they are God`s people?(research)

3)What should they do if it remains on the third day?

b.What happens if they do eat it on the third day?(3reasons)

4)What can't the children of Israel do?(10things)

5)Shall the wages of thy servant abide with them all night?

6)What does the word stumblingblock mean?

7)How shall they judge their neighbor?

8)How can we love are neighbors?

9)What year could they eat of the fruit?

10)What does the word mar mean in verse 277

11)What does the word prostitute mean?

12)What shall they do unto the stranger that dwelleth with them?

Chapter 20

I)What shall happen if they give their child unto Molech?(how shall they die?)

2)What shall happen to someone if they curse their parents?

3)What shall happen if someone commits adultery with another man's wife?

b.What about if they lie with their mother?

4)What will be the punishment ifthey take a wife and her mother?

5)What if someone lies with a beast what happens to them?

6)How will someone that lies with their uncle's wife be punished?

7)What happens to a person that has a familiar spirit or is a wizard?

Chapter 21
1)Why can't the priest's be defiled?

2)What two woman can't they take as wives?(2kinds)

3)What is the punishment for a daughter of a priest if she goes a whoring around?

4)What are the things a person who is anointed high priest not do?(6things)

5)Who are the people that has a blemish that can't offer the bread of his God?(12people)

Chapter 22

I)Why can't they go unto the holy things with uncleanness?

2)When shall they be pronounced clean?

3)Who shall eat of the holy thing besides the priest?(2people)

4)What if someone eats it unwillingly?

Chapter 23

1)Narne the first feast they shall perform.

2)Narne the second feast they shall perform,

3)Narne the third feast they shall perform(describe what they should do)

4)N~e the fourth feast they shall perform(describe what they should do)

5)What is the fifth feast they shall perform?(describe it)

6)What is the sixth feast they shall perform?(describe it)

7)What is the seventh feast they shall perform?(describe it)

8)What is the eighth feast they shall perform?(describe it)

Chapter 24
1) Why should they bring pure olive oil for the light?

2) What did the son of an israelitish woman and the father an Egyptian do?

b. What was his punishment?

Chapter 25
1) What shall they not do on the Sabbath day in verse 5?(2things)

2) What shall they do on the tenth day of the seventh month in the fiftieth year?

3) What shall the fiftieth year be to them?

b. What can't they do on this year?

4)How will the Lord provide for them to eat on the seventh year?

5)What did the Lord say in verse 23?

6)How must a man redeem that which he sold?

7)Why can't the fields of the suburbs be sold?

8)What a man's brother be sold unto him what shall he be?

9)Who shall be their bondman or bondwoman?

1O)How does the day ofrest apply to us today?

Chapter 26

1) What will the Lord do if they keep his commandments? (7 things)

2) In verse 13 what has the Lord done for them?

3) What will the Lord do unto them if they don't obey his commandments? (5 things)

4) What will the Lord do unto them in verse 19? (3 things)

5) What shall the do unto the people?

b. Where shall they live?

6) What if they confess their inquities unto the Lord when they are in the enemies land?

Chapter 27

I)How much do they give unto the Lord if they make a vow?

b.What if they were 5 to 20 years old?

2)How much tithe of the land is the Lord's?

Bible Study Questions in Numbers

Chapter 1

1)What was the name of the head of the tribe of Rueben?

2)Name the head of the tribe of Simeon.

3)Name the head of the tribe of Judah.

4)Name the head of the tribe of Issachar.

5)Name the head ofthe tribe of Zebulun.

6)Name the head ofthe tribe of Ephraim.

7)Name the head of the tribe of Manasseh.

8)Name the head of the tribe of Benjamin.

9)Name the head of the tribe of Dan.

10)Name the head of the tribe of Asher.

Il)Name the head of the tribe of Gad.

12)Name the head of the tribe of Naphtali.

13)How many were there from 20 years old and up that were able to go to war?

14) Were the Levites numbered with them?

15) What did the Lord appoint the Levites to do?

Chapter 2

I) Who shall camp on the east side toward the risiug of the sun? (3tribes)

b. How many are there all together iu this camp?

2) Who shall camp on the south side?

b. How many are there all together in this camp?

3) Who shall camp on the west side?

b.How many are there all together in this camp?

4)Who shall camp on the north side?

b.How many are there all together in this camp?

5)What pattern did this make?

Chapter 3
l)Why did the Lord take the Levites instead ofthe firstborn of every tribe?

2)Name the sons of Gershon.

3)Name the sons of Kohath.

4)Name the sons of Merari.

5)How many are there from a month and up in the family of Gershon?

b.Who is the chief of the family of Gershon?

c.What are they in charge of?

6)How many are there from a month and up in the family of Kohath?

b:Who is the chief of the family of Kohath?

e.What are they in charge of?

7)How many are there from a month and up in the family of Merari?

b.Who is the ehief of the family of Merari?

e.What are they in charge of?

Chapter 4

l)How old shall the sons of Kohath be able to work?

2)What shall Aaron and his sons do first?

3)What shall the sons of Kohath do?

b.What will happen if they touch any of the holy things?

4)What shall they not do in verse 20?

5)What shall the Gershonites do for their service?

6)Who shall be in charge of them?

7)What shall the Merarites do for their service?

8)How many were there all together that did service?

Chapter 5

I)Who shall the children ofIsrael put outside the camp?(3types ofpeople)

2)What shall a man do after he is guilty of committing a sin?(4things)

3)What if a woman doesn't lay with another man and cause her husband to be jealous?

4)What if she did defile her husband and lay with another man?

Chapter 6
I)What is the first vow he will take to be a nazarite?(7things)

2)What is the second vow he will take to be a nazarite?

3)What is the other thing he should separate himself from?

4)When a person dies beside him then he's defiled,what shall he do?

5)What shall Aaron tell the children of lsrael?(4things)

Chapter 7

1) What the princes over each tribe offer?

2) Did the Kohathites get any of the offering?

3) Who was the first to offer, and what did he offer?

4) Who was the second to offer, and what did he offer?

5) Who was the third to offer , and what did he offer?

6) Who was the fourth to offer, and what did he offer?

7) Who was the fifth to offer, and what did he offer?

8)Who was the sixth to offer,and what did he offer?

9)Who was the seventh to offer,and what did he offer?

10)Who was the eighth to offer,and what did he offer?

11)Who was the nineth to offer,and what did he offer?

12)Who was the tenth to offer ,and what did he offer?

13)Who was the eleventh to offer,and what did he offer?

14)Who was the twelveth to offer,and what did he offer?

15) What did Moses hear in verse 89?

Chapter 8

I) How shall the Levites cleanse themselves? (3things)

2) What shall the Levites that are over fifty do?

Chapter 9

I) What did the men that were defiled by a dead body tell Moses?

2) Shall they keep the Passover?

3) What did they do at the commandment of the Lord?

Chapter 10

I)What shall they use the trumpets for?(2things)

2)Shall they sound an alarm when they shall be assembled together?

3)What did Moses tell Hobab?

4)What did Moses say in verse 35?

Chapter 11

I)What did the Lord do unto the children of Israel?

2)What did Moses tell the Lord?(5questions)

3)What did the Lord tell him in verse 17?

4)What did the seventy elders do when the spirit of the Lord rested on them?

5)When did the Lord put a plague on them?

Chapter 12

1)What did Aaron and Miriam say in verse 2?(2questions)

2)What did the Lord tell Aaron and Miriam?

3)What happened to Miriam after the cloud left?

Chapter 13

1)Name the first spy that shall spy out the land of Canaan.

2)Who was the second spy?

3)Who was the third spy?

4)Who was the fourth spy?

5)Who was the fifth spy?

6)Who was the sixth spy?

7)Who was the seventh spy?

8)Who was the eighth spy?

9)Who was the nineth spy?

10)Who was the tenth spy?

11)Who was the eleventh spy?

12)Who was the twelveth spy?

13)What did he tell the spies?(4things)

14)What was the information they gave Moses?

15)What did Caleb say?

16)What did the rest of them say?

Chapter 14
1)What did they say in verse 3?(2questions)

2)What were they going to do?

3)What did Joshua and Caleb tell them?(6thing s)

4)What did the Lord tell Moses about the children of Israel?(2questions)

5)How did Moses describe the Lord in verse 18?(5things)

6)What does verse 21 mean?

7) Who shall enter into the land the Lord promised them?

8) What happened to the men that gave a bad report?

Chapter 15

1) What shall they do when they eat the bread of the land?

2) What shall a person do if they were ignorance?

3) What if a person do it presumptuously?

4) What did the Lord tell Moses that they should do with the man that picked up sticks on the Sabbath?

5)Why should the children of Israel put fringes in their garments?

Chapter 16
1)Who is Korah' s father?

b.Who is his grandfather?

c.Who is his greatgrandfather?

2)What did Korah tell Moses and Aaron?

3)What did Moses tell Korah and the men with him?

b.What he tell them to do?

4)What did he tell the rest of the children of Israel to do?

5)What happened to the men that was against Moses and Aaron?

6)What shall Eleazar do with the censers of the sinners?

7)What did the Lord do unto the people that murmured unto him about Korah and the other men?

b.How many people died of them?

Chapter 17
1)What shall the princes bring unto Moses?

2)What shall be the reason for the rods?(2reasons)

3)Who 's rod budded and what did they do with the rod?

Chapter 1 8

I)What shall Aaron and his sons bear?(2things)

2)How are the Levites a gift to them?

3)What shall be theirs of the most holy things?(4things)

4)What else shall be theirs?(5things)

5)What did the Lord tell Aaron in verse 20?

6)Who shall get the tithes of the children of Israel?

Chapter 19

I) What should the red heifer not have to be sacrificed?(3things)

2) What shall the priest who burned have to do?

3) What shall the clean man do with the ashes and what shall this be called?

4) What shall a clean person do?(8things)

Chapter 20

1) Where was Miriam buried?

2) Why did they say it was an evil place?

3) What did the Lord tell Moses to do?

4) Did Moses do what the Lord told him to do?

5) What was Moses and Aaron's punishment?

6) What did they tell the king of Edom in verse 17?

7) Why didn't he let them pass?

8) Where did Aaron die?

Chapter 21
1) What did the king Arad do?(2things)

2) What vow did Israel vow?

3)What did the Lord punish them with because of their murmurings?

4)How shall the children ofIsraellive after being bit by the snakes?

5)How shall the children of Israel live after being bit by snakes?

6)What did the children of Israel do unto Sihon,king of the Amorites?

7)What did the Lord tell Moses in verse 34?

Chapter 22
l)What did Moab say unto the elders ofMidian?

2)What Balak want Balaam to do?

3) What Balaam tell the messengers of Balak?

4) Did Balaam do what God wanted him to do?

5) What did the donkey see the first time?

b. What did the donkey do unto Balaam the second time?

c. What did the donkey say unto Balaam?

6) What did the sngel of the Lord tell Balaam?

7) What the angel ofthe Lord tell him to do?

Chapter 23
1)What is the first prophesy he told Balak?(reasons)

2)What was the second prophesy he told Balak?

Chapter 24
1)What happened when Balaam seen the tents of Israel?

2)How did he describe the children of Israel?

3)Who is he talking about in verse 7?

b.How did he describe him?

4)What did he prophesy the fourth time unto Balak?

5) What was the fifth prophesy he told?

6) What was the sixth prophesy he told?

7) Wbat was the seventh prophesy he told?

Chapter 25

1) What did Moses tell the judges to do?

2) Wbat did Phinehas do unto the man and the midianitish woman?

3) How many died in the plague?

4) Wbat did the Lord do unto Phinehas?

5) Wbat was the name of the man who died and what tribe was he from?

b. Wbat was the name of the woman?

Chapter 26
1) Name the people in the tribe of Reuben that were able to go to war.

2) Name the people in the tribe of Simeon.

3) Name the people in the tribe of Gad.

4) Name the people in the tribe of Judah.

5) Name the people in the tribe of Issachar.

6)Name the people in the tribe of Zebulun.

7)Name the people in the tribe of Manasseh.

8)Name the people in the tribe of Ephraim,

9)Name the people in the tribe of Benjamin.

IO)Name the people in the tribe of Dan.

11)Name the people in the tribe of Asher.

12)Name the people in the tribe of Naphtali.

13) What did the Lord tell them in verse 54?

Chapter 27
I) Name the daughters of Zelophehad.

2) What did they want Moses to give unto them?

3) Who shall succeed Moses?(describe what he shall do)?

Chapter 28
1) When was this made a continual burnt offering ?

2) When shall they offer a burnt offering ?

Chapter 29
1) What is this called on seventh month and the first day?

2) What shall they do in verse 5?

3) What did he tell them in verse 39?

Chapter 30
1) What shall he do if he swear to keep an oath unto the Lord?

2) What are the four reasons for a woman who makes a vow?

3) What shall happen to the husband in verse 15?

Chapter 31

1) What did Moses tell them to do and how many went?

2) What did Phinebas take with him?

3) Name the five kings of Midian that were killed.

4) What did they also do unto Midian?(4things)

5) Why was Moses made at them?

6) What did they do to the captives?

Chapter 32

1) What did the children of Reuben and Gad ask Moses in verse 5?

2)What was the questions he asked them?(2questions)

3)What else did he tell them?

4)What did they tell Moses they would do?

5)What did he say to them in verse 23?

6)Name the cities that the tribe of Gad built.

7)Name the cities that the tribe of Reuben built.

8)Name the cities that half the tribe of Manasseh built.

Chapter 33

1) What was the places that they went to?(32places)

2) How old was Aaron when he died?

3) What was other places they went to?(8places)

4) What will happen if they don't drive them out of the land?

Chapter 34

1) What shall be their south border?

2) What shall be their west border?

3) What shall be their north border?

4)What shall be their east border?

5)Who shall divide the Iands?(2men)

6)Narne the prince of Judah.

7)Narne the prince of Sirneon.

8)Name the prince of Benjamin.

9)Name the prince of Dan.

1O)Name the prince of Manasseh.

I I)Name the prince of Ephraim

12)Name the prince of Zebulun.

13)Name the prince of Issachar.

14)Name the prince of Asher.

15)Name the prince of Naphtali.

Chapter 35
1)What shall the children of Israel give unto the Levites?(2things)

2)What does it say in verse 8?

3)What shall these cities be for?

4)What shall happen to the murderer in verse 21?

5)Shall the revenger of blood be guilty if he slays the murderer that gets out of the city of refuge?

6)Why should they not have any satisfaction for the murderer?

Chapter 36

1)What did the tribe of Manasseh tell Moses about the daughters of Zelophehad?

2)What did Moses say to the people about this?

Bible Study Questions in Deuteronomy

Chapter 1

1) What does the word Deuteronomy mean?(research)

2) Name the five cities that they were between.

3) When did Moses speak unto the children of children of Israel?(m/d/y)

4) What did he tell them in verse 8?(2things)

5) What does cumbrance mean?(research)

6) How was the judges to judge the children of Israel?(4ways)

7)What were the things they told the people so they would murmur against the Lord?(3things)

8)What will the Lord give unto Caleb?

9)What did the Lord tell the ones who murmured?

Chapter 2

1)What did the Lord tell them when they pass through Esau`s land(3things)

2)What did the Lord tell them about Moab?(3things)

3)What does the word giants mean?(research)

4)What did the Lord tell them about Ammon?(3things)

Chapter 3

1)How many cities did the children of Israel destroy that was Og`s?

2)How large was the bedstaed of Og?

3)Who is lair ,and what land did he possess?

4)Who is Machir, and what city did he possess?

5)What did he give the Reubenites&Gadites?

6)What did Moses tell the Lord?(3things)

7)What did the Lord tell Moses?

Chapter 4

1) What did Moses tell them in verse 2?

2) What did he tell them in verse 6?

3) What questions did Moses tell them?(2questions)

4) What did he tell them in verse 9?(4reasons)

5) What are the things they can't make any graven image of?(5things)

6) What did he compare Egypt to in verse 20?

7) What is the Lord?(2things)

8)What did he tell them in verse 27?

9)What are the three cities of refuge?

Chapter 5
I)Who does the Lord show mercy unto ?(2reaso05)

b.How many people?

2)What question did they give?

3)What did the Lord desire of them?

Chapter 6

1)What will happen if they observe the commandments?(2thing s)

2)How shall they love the Lord?(3things)

3)What shall they do with the words?(I Othings)

4)What shall he give them if they obey?(3things)

5)What shall thy son say unto them?

6)What will be their reply?(3things)

Chapter 7

1)What did Moses tell them?(5things)

2)What did he tell them in verse 5?(2things)

3)What will the Lord do for them if the keep his commandments?(12things)

4)Will they consume the nations all at once?

5)Why cann't they bring the abomination in their house?

Chapter 8
1)Why shall they remember that they wondered in the wilderness for forty years?(4things)

2)What does man live by instead of bread?

3)What will the land have in it?(I 7things)

4)What will they say in verse 17 that will make God judge them?

5)What will happen if they don't keep his commandments?

Chapter 9

1)What shall they not speak?

2)How shall they possess the land, and how shall they not possess the land?(4ways)

3)What did they do near mount Horeb to make God angry?

4)Where else did they provoke the Lord?(3places)

5)What did Moses pray unto the Lord?(2things)

Chapter 10

1)What did the Lord tell Moses?(2things)

2)What is Jotbath called?

3)Who is Levi's inheritance?

4)What did the Lord tell Moses?

5)What does the Lord require of them?(5things)

6)What did the Lord tell them to do in verse 16?

Chapter 11

1)What didn't the children of them not see?(6things)

2)When are the eyes of the Lord on the land where they are going to possess?

3)What shall the Lord give them ifthe serve hirn&keep his commandments?(2things)

4)What shall be theirs if they do what the Lord told them to do?

Chapter 12
I)What shall they do unto the nations?(8things)

2)What shall they do unto the place that God chooses for them ?(9things)

3)Who shall rejoice before the Lord?(6people)

4)What shall they not eat before their gates?(7things)

5)Who shall the people not forsake?

6)Why shall they not eat the blood?

7)What does verse 32 mean?(in your own opinion)

Chapter 13

I)What shall they do if the prophet tells them to follow other gods?

2)Why will God allow them to speak those words?

3)What will happen to that prophet or dreamer?

4)What shall they do &not do unto them that entice them to worship other gods?(6things)

5)What shall they do with the city that worships other gods?(4things)

Chapter 14

I) What shall they not do unto themselves?(2things)

2)What shall they eat?(10things)

3)What shall they not eat in verse 7 and why?(3things)

4)What shall they not eat in verse 8 and why?

5)What shall they eat and not eat ofthat in the waters?

6)What shall they not eat of the birds?(21things)

7)What shall they do to the thing that dieth?(2things)

8)What shall they tithe?

9)What shall they do ifit is to far to take it?

Chapter 15
I)What shall they do after seven years?

2)What is it they do in verse 2?

3)What about the foreigner?

4)What will happen in verse 6?(4things)

5) Who shall they open their hand to?(3people)

6) What shall they not do with the firstlings of their herd or flock?

7) What shall they not sacrifice unto the Lord?(4things)

Chapter 16
1) What did he do for them in the month of Abib?

2) Shall they sacrifice with their gates ?

3) How shall they keep the feast of weeks?

4) How many times shall the males appear before the Lord?

5)Who shall give if he is able?

6)What shall the judges not do?(3things)

7)What does a gift do?(2things)

Chapter 17

I) What shall they do to the people who worship other gods?(2things)

2)How many witnesses can he then be put to death?

b.How many witnesses can he not be put to death?

3)How shall they be put to death?(2ways)

4)What shall they do if a matter be to hard to judge?

5)What then shall the judges do ?(3things)

6)What if that man doesn't listen to the priests or judge?

7)What will they do when they are in the land?

8)What shall he do and not do?(6things)

Chapter 18
1)What shall they give the priests ?(7things)

2)What shall they not do when they enter the land?(9things)

3)Who is the Prophet in verse 15?

4)What did Moses tell the Lord?(2things)

5)What will the Prophet do?(2things)

6)How shall they know if it was the Lord that spoke?

Chapter 19
1)What shall they do in verse 2)

2)What shall they do if they love the Lord&keep his commandments?

3)What shall they do and not do unto someone that killeth his in haterd?(2things)

4) What shall they do if a false witness rise up against someone?

Chapter 20
1) What shall they not be afraid of? (3things)

2) What shall the priests tell them? (6things)

3) What shall the officers tell them? (6things)

4) What else shall the officers tell them? (2things)

5) What shall happen if the city is open to peace? (2things)

6) What shall they do un to the males in the city?

b.What shall they do unto the women,children,and flocks?

7)Why shall they not cut down the trees?

Chapter 21

I) What shall they do if a man was slain in the field and noone knows who did it?(4things)

2)What shall they say unto the priests?(2things)

3)What if a man desires a woman of the captives to be his wife?(5things)

4)What if he doesn`t want the woman?(4things)

5)What should a man do to the son that was the firstborn, but was of the wife he hated?

6) What shall they do unto a son that is rebellious?

7) What shall they do to the man after they hang on a tree?

Chapter 22
1) What shall they do unto a brother's ox?

2) What else shall they give unto their brother?(3things)

3) What shall a woman or a man do in verse 5?

4) What shall they do if they build a house?

5) What are the other things they shalt not do?(3things)

6) What shall the elders do unto the man that hateth his wife a say is not a virgin but her father proves she is a virgin?

7) What if the husband telleth the truth about his wife?

8) What shall they do someone that layeth with another man's wife?

Chapter 23
1) Who shall not enter unto the congregation? (5people)

2) Who shall enter unto the congregation? (3people)

3) Why shall their camp be clean?

4) What shall they not do with a servant that has escaped?

5)What shall there not be in the daughters&sons of Israel?

6)When they make a vow unto the Lord what shall they not bring?(3things)

7)What shall they do if they do vow?

Chapter 24
I)Shall her former take the woman as his wife again?

2)What shall a man do or not do if he has a new wife?(4things)

3)What shall they not do unto a hired servant?

4)What shall be for the stranger in the camp?(3things)

Chapter 25

1) What shall the judges do unto them that have controversy?(2things)

2) How many stripes shall they give him if he worthy to be beaten?

3) What shall a brother's wife tell the elders ?

4) What shall the elders to&say unto the brother?(3things)

5) What shall they have in verse 15?

6) What shall they not blot out?

Chapter 26

1) What shall they in verse 2?(4things)

2)What shall they say before the Lord?(9things)

Chapter 27

1)What shall they do when they pass over Jordan?(3things)

2)Who shall bless the people on mount Gershim?(6tribes)

3)Who shall curse the people on mount Ebal?(6tribes)

4)What are the curses that will be put on them that sin against God?(12curses)

Chapter 28

1)What will the Lord do if they observe to obey all the commandments?

2)What will be the blessings that God shall give them?(9blessings)

3)Shall the people of the earth be afraid of Israel?

4)What shall the do unto them in verse 12?(4things)

5)What will be the curses that God shall give them?(8curses)

6)What shall cleave unto them until they are off the land?

7)What will the Lord smite them with?(7things)

8)What shalt their carcass be meat for?(2things)

9)What else will the Lord smite them with?(4things)

10)What else will the Lord smite them with?(3things)

II)Shall their children be given unto other people?

12)What shall the Lord do unto them&and their king?

13)What shall they be unto other nations?(3things)

14)What nation is the Lord talking about in verses 49,50?

15)What shall the Lord do unto them in verse 64?

Chapter 29

1) What have the Lord given unto them?(3things)

2) Who else does he make these covenant for?(2people)

3) What does gall&wormwood mean?(research)

4) What will the nations say?(2questions)

5) What belongs unto God and to us?

Chapter 30

1) What shall they do when the blessings& and curses come upon them?(3things)

2)What will the Lord do unto them?

3)What will the Lord make them?

4)Where is and isn't the word of the Lord ?(4places)

5)What will happen to them if they don`t love him and worship him?(2things)

6)What does the Lord want them to do?

Chapter 31
I)How old is Moses in verse 2?

2)What is the things he told them?(6things)

3)What shall the priests do at the end of seven years?

4)What did the Lord tell Moses in verse 16?

5)What did the Lord tell in verse 19?

Chapter 32
1)What shall his speech do?(3things)

2)How does Moses describe God?(5things)

3)What was the questions he said in verse 6?(3questions)

4)How did the Lord keep them in verse 10?

5)Who is it talking about in verse 15?

6)What did the Lord say unto them in verse 20?(4things)

7)What would have them to do?(3things)

8)What question did he ask them in verse 34?

9)What does the word whet mean?(research)

1O)What did Moses tell them in verse 46?

11)What did the Lord tell him?

Chapter 33

1)What did he say unto Reuben?(2things)

2)What was Judah's blessing ?(2things)

3)What was Benjamin's blessing ?(3things)

4)What was Joseph's blessing?(8things)

5)What was Zebulun's blessing?

6)What is Issachar`s blessing?

7)What was Gad' s blessing?(6things)

8)What was Dan's blessing?(2things)

9)What was Naphtali' s blessing?(3things)

1O)What was Asher 's blessing?(5things)

Chapter 34

I)What did the Lord tell Moses?

2)Where did they bury Moses?

3)Has anybody found his body?

4)Was there a prophet like Moses?

Many people don't take the Bible off the shelf and open it up and read it because they say they don't understand what it says. When you study the Bible with this book, even if you haven't ever read or studied the Word of God before; it will help you get a little basic knowledge in the Word of God. I wrote this Study Guide for people who have just got saved or for young people. When anyone uses the Expositor's Study Bible along with this study they will find some of the answers are in the commentary part.

Today there are many study guides out there that provide some help for you, but this Study Guide breaks down every chapter in the first five books of the Bible. I will give you a sample in this Study Guide. (It is not just called the Law, but also the Tora and the Pentateuch).

So I hope you find this study to help you learn the first five books of the Bible, and maybe you can use it to teach others who want to learn more about the Bible.